To Teach Is to Touch Lives Forever

Written, edited, and compiled by
Marc Anello, Claudine Gandolfi,
S. M. Scott, and Virginia Unser

Illustrated by Barbara Chiantia

PETER PAUPER PRESS, INC.
WHITE PLAINS, NEW YORK

For Louise Bachelder,
English and French teacher extraordinaire

Original artwork
copyright © 1998 Barbara Chiantia
licensed by Wild Apple Licensing

Book design by Arlene Greco

Text copyright © 1998
Peter Pauper Press, Inc.
202 Mamaroneck Avenue
White Plains, NY 10601
All rights reserved
ISBN 0-88088-073-2
Printed in China
7 6 5 4 3 2 1

To Teach Is to Touch Lives Forever

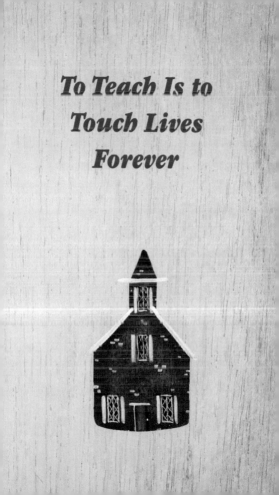

Introduction

In the town where I live there is a schoolhouse that sits on a gently sloping hill. The town has grown several times over since that schoolhouse was built, and a few blocks to the north of it a complex of modern brick buildings now houses an elementary, a middle, and a high school.

Not so long ago there was a notion among some of the folks who govern the town to take the schoolhouse down and sell the small parcel of land on which it stood. It would take too much of your time to tell the story of the reaction by many here among us to that particular proposal.

But allow me, if you will, to tell you how it became "The Old School House Ice Cream Parlor."

Jesse and Linda Pierce sold ice cream and other snacks during the warm weather from a mobile truck. It occurred to the Pierces that in order to continue to make a living doing what they enjoyed they needed a permanent year-round site from which to sell their treats. They bought the schoolhouse and the land from the town to convert it into an ice cream parlor and cafe. In the course of cleaning up and remodeling, they left in place the old blackboards and some of the desks that were in decent condition—to maintain the schoolhouse's ambiance.

One Saturday night while closing up they noticed that a patron had written on a blackboard, "On this spot Mrs. Pell taught me well, and now I am a better person for my time spent here." The Pierces realized that within these walls numerous teachers and students had shared in an experience that had in some fashion touched them forever. They left the inscription intact. Over the ensuing weeks other patrons, taking their cue from the ditty about Mrs. Pell, added their own recollections about having gone to school or taught at the schoolhouse. The Pierces began to encourage these expressions. When the blackboards became full they carefully copied the sentiments onto 4" x 6" cards and arranged them on the walls. They cleared the blackboards and, to their delight, new epigrams, poems, and quotes began to be written and posted.

And so it occurred to me, while enjoying one of the Pierces' delightful ice cream confections, that a book of sentiments and appreciation about the magic of teaching and learning would be enjoyed by a wide audience—and here it is!

S. M. SCOTT

I feel full from the daily feast that the baker prepares. I am grateful to the bus driver on my route who (almost) always arrives on time. I am safer for the vigilance of the police officer in my local precinct. I am in better health for the care of my doctor. *I am eternally in awe of the teacher who taught me to learn, and has made everything that I do possible.*

WHEELER MANVILLE

Teachers can change lives with just the right mix of chalk and challenges.

JOYCE A. MYERS

For teachers the biggest thrill is to have a former student walk into the classroom years later and say how much the experience with that teacher meant to him. This is what gives meaning to his work and confirms him as an educator.

MYRON BRENTON

Most people can remember great teachers from their own years in school—caring adults who excited youthful imaginations, or inspired hard work and achievement.

LOUIS V. GERSTNER

Who is not able to recall the impact of some particular teacher—an enthusiast, a devotee of a point of view, a disciplinarian whose ardor came from love of a subject, a playful but serious mind? There are many images, and they are precious

JEROME S. BRUNNER

To reach a child's mind a teacher must capture his heart. Only if a child feels right can he think right.

HAIM G. GINNOTT

Mr. Drake could speak the language like no other teacher I've ever had. He read Shakespeare aloud to the class, and the silence was profound. Who ever heard of that in a high school English classroom? You were barely aware that he was reciting poetry; it sounded so natural.

Now that I've tried to write in blank verse myself, I realize how difficult it is to achieve that effortless quality. He made the tragedies seem like soap operas, which, of course, they are. The comedies he reduced to pure slapstick. To this day, I believe that it's the best way to grab the

attention of a bunch of teenagers.
We learned in spite of ourselves.

CAROLYN DUFF

If the heavens were all parchment,
and the trees of the forests all pens,
and every human being were a
scribe, it would be impossible to
record all that I have learned from
my teachers.

ATTRIBUTED TO JOHANAN BEN ZAKKAI

Teaching is an act that, when done well, fully occupies the present moment, but also always with an eye on the future.

DAVID T. HANSEN

To learn and to teach, one must have an awareness of leaving something behind while reaching toward something new, and this kind of awareness must be linked to imagination.

MAXINE GREENE

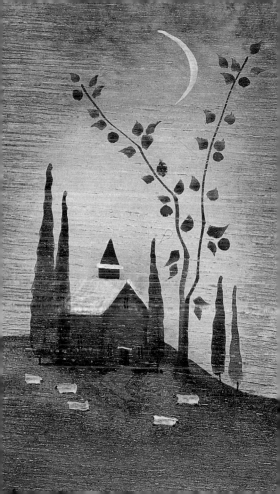

Everyone who remembers his own educational experience remembers teachers, not methods and techniques.

SIDNEY HOOK

One looks back with appreciation to the brilliant teachers, but with gratitude to those who touched our human feelings. The curriculum is so much necessary raw material, but warmth is the vital element for the growing plant and for the soul of the child.

CARL JUNG

I am quite sure that in the hereafter
she will take me by the hand and
lead me to my proper seat.

BERNARD BARUCH,
recalling one of his early teachers

The relationship between teacher
and student . . . is by no means
bounded by the classroom . . .
[A]nyone who has taught for any
length of time can, I suspect, sense
the power he has over his students.
This power is a sacred trust.

JOSEPH EPSTEIN

I was so very scared the first day at my new school. My momma tried to keep me calm. She soothed me as well as she could. She said, "Charlene, you'll be O.K. This school here is a nice place and that teacher looks like a fine one. I know you'll feel like a duck rollin' in water in no time." I knew my momma was saying what she thought was right, and I believed that she believed it too, but I was still scared and I'm sure my knees were shaking. Then a pretty woman with spectacles hanging on a string came to the classroom door and took me sweetly and firmly by the hand, and she said. "Why, you must be Charlene Webb. I am so happy to have you here in my class." I just knew that pretty woman, whose name turned out to be Mrs. Shaw, would not lie to me. I believed her with all my heart.

And so I have always kept my eyes sharp on the first day of school each September for the child who looks a little extra scared, a little more apprehensive than the other children. And when I spot the one, I walk over to her and take her hand in mine so that she knows I'm going to keep a special eye out for her.

CHARLENE WEBB ALTON

Teaching is primarily a matter of love.
The rest is, at best, ornamentation.

WILLIAM AYERS

She (Lois Van Epps) was the kind of
dream teacher a lot of kids want to
have in their lives. More than any of
us, she always stayed in contact with
her old students, to whom she was
truly a friend.

PEG FISK

I don't know exactly why but we all thought that Mrs. Larune was kind of unusual. Maybe it was because she had a bump on her nose, or seemed to wear black more often than any adult we knew. Kids at school used to say things like, "That Mrs. Larune is a goon," or, "You know Mrs. Larune is a witch and she only comes out at the full moon." Around Halloween kids said, "I sure wish I knew where Mrs. Larune lived. I bet you it's a run-down spooky house. We could ring her doorbell and hide in the bushes to see her come out holding her broom."

One Saturday afternoon while I was walking to the ball field to meet some friends I saw a woman, dressed in a white T-shirt and jeans, working on a flat tire on her Chevy. I did a quadruple take when I realized that this was either Mrs. Larune or her identical twin. She had the jack in place and was getting some pretty good lift into the bumper. "Vincent D'Orio?" "Yes, maam." "Do you think that you could help me loosen the lug nuts on this rim?" I wasn't sure what to say and I wasn't sure how she knew my name. When she saw me hesitate, she said, "Vincent, come on, I won't bite." I felt really dumb, but managed to help her remove the flat and put on the spare. All the time she was talking to me plain regular, as regular as anyone I'd ever heard. I realized that she was a very nice person. When the spare was on and the flat was secure in her trunk, she asked if I needed a ride. Without thinking I said, "Sure, I'm just going to Farrow field, is that O.K.?" She assured me that it was.

The guys didn't notice how I got to the field and I didn't say a word. We played ball until dark, and then I walked home. I know that it sounds trite but, by being exactly who she was, Mrs. Larune taught me in the subtlest of ways that teachers are people too.

VINCENT D'ORIO

To teach is to be full of hope.

LARRY CUBAN

I'll never forget my first semester in college. I was miserable and felt so alone. No one seemed to really understand me . . . no one, except Monsieur Poirier. He and I both believed in an independent Quebec . . . two Separatists in an ocean of Federalists. Two days after the Separatists lost the referendum on sovereignty Monsieur Poirier decided that everyone in the class should talk about what they were experiencing and their reactions to the vote on the referendum. I just lost it. Right there in the middle of the classroom. I cried and cried and cried. For the first time in my life I had the courage to speak my mind in front of 30 people. I told my classmates things that I had never had the courage to admit to myself before that day. Monsieur Poirier ended class early, and he came over to where I stood and gave me a huge hug. Tears were streaming down his face. He told me that what I did took a lot of courage and not to give up. He gave me hope. He gave me the courage to dream again. Had he not been there I would most likely have changed schools, given up hope, and resigned myself to believing that dreams don't come true.

MARIE-HÉLÈNE GRATTON

Dear Aunt Thea,

We have a new teacher who comes to our class on Fridays. She's an artist like you. She shows us all different kinds of paints that we can use. Last week we used pastels, and I got to blend them with my fingers. That was fun! She taught me all the colors in the rainbow. She also showed us how to paint with feathers, and pieces of grass, and a sponge. Did you know that you could squash up rocks and make paints? The American Indians did that. I really like art class now. I hope I can be an artist, too, when I grow up.

KARLA WILLIAMS

If education doesn't prepare the young to educate themselves throughout their lives, then it is a failure, no matter what else it may seem to accomplish.

SYDNEY J. HARRIS

Spoon feeding in the long run teaches us nothing but the shape of the spoon.

E. M. FORSTER

It was a teacher who inspired me. It was a very horribly cold day, as it can be in Alabama, and we were just sitting there feeling sad and dejected, and our teacher told us that she couldn't help us fight the horrible conditions that were around us but she could show us the way out. She showed us the world of books, that you can survive through books.

EVELYN JENKINS GUNN

I used to wonder whether, with a name like "Wall," Mr. Wall ever got crank phone calls. It's just like a bunch of 12-year-old kids to do that. Mr. Wall was a patient man. I never heard him shout at a student, although he did ban me from participating in a science experiment because I made too many wisecracks. Mr. Wall taught us that our opinions mattered, and that our actions bore consequences. He would listen ever so patiently to the tumbling litanies of his preteen charges. An amateur geologist, he took us on rock-collecting expeditions. I still love picking up stones and examining them, and putting them in my pocket. My little daughter now does the same. And one day soon I will teach my daughter another of Mr. Wall's lessons: that, like the stones on the beach, we are all unique and of value.

STEPHANIE DOYLE

My heart is singing for joy this morning. A miracle has happened! The light of understanding has shone upon my little pupil's mind, and behold, all things are changed!

ANNIE SULLIVAN

As a calling teaching is a moral enterprise, a form of testifying for the good, and a sacred trust.

CRAIG KRIDEL

[T]he wonderful uniqueness and
potential of each and every child in
the room . . . is the sight that brings
most teachers to the classroom in the
first place, and which inspires their
best efforts and their commitment to
their calling.

LAUNA ELLISON

Good teaching cannot be reduced to
a technique. Good teaching comes
from the identity and integrity of the
teacher.

PARKER PALMER

Miss Glover wore "go-go" boots, and taught me how to spell "communication." She also provided me with my earliest and most invaluable lesson—on grace. For months I'd been secretly, agonizingly in love with her. I waved my hand with zealous fervor every time a messenger was needed to go to the office. I imagined myself on a religious pilgrimage as I walked up the center aisle of the classroom, took the slip from her manicured fingertips, and inhaled her fragrance.

During the final field trip of the school year, I was allowed to hold

Miss Glover's hand, for I was "buddy-less." My eight-year-old hand growing moist, I whispered, "Miss Glover, I think you're beautiful." She didn't blush or titter. She didn't even crack a smile. "Thank you, Edward," was all she said, and she gave me a brief, approving look. We walked on in silence.

EDWARD REYNOLDS

We have touched lives. That's what matters. That's what we remember.

PATRICIA SULLIVAN RAMSEY,
retired teacher

The best teacher is one who, through establishing a personal relation, frees the student to learn. Learning can only take place in the student, and the teacher can only create the conditions for learning. The atmosphere created by a good interpersonal relationship is the major condition for learning.

C. H. PATTERSON

If you become a lifetime learner along with your students, if you join with them in not knowing, not being sure, the excitement of unfolding is yours as well as theirs. Unfolding children can be the teachers for unfolding parents and educators. Lifetime learning is like lifetime living. It begins with an inner energy source and grows richer in our listening and speaking.

ELAINE YOUNG

There are people who walked into my office and I took one look at them and spoke with them for five minutes and I could say, This is going to be a great teacher. You just get the feeling from their intelligence, their enthusiasm, their willingness to learn—their excitement about being a learner themselves. . . . There is no doubt in my mind that there are certain qualities that individuals have that might make them a great teacher. And there is the part that has to be learned.

DR. THOMAS S. BUTERA

The . . . task for the teacher is to devise situations in which the young will move from the habitual and the ordinary and consciously undertake a search.

MAXINE GREENE

It's possible we could teach kids anything. I get them to live the concepts. My job is to push them. I want 30 Rocky Balboas, 30 people who are thirsting to learn.

JOSEPH L. VICARI

It takes years to learn how to teach well, and even then one never learns once and for all. Teaching is not like driving a car or adding a column of figures. . . . Like any craft, one learns teaching by practicing it and by finding models, other teachers whose practice one admires and can study.

HERBERT R. KOHL

Everywhere the task of teaching is
the same— this lighting of sparks,
this setting aflame—and everywhere
it is carried on differently. This is the
inherent fascination of the subject.

JOSEPH EPSTEIN

In the future, we shall measure our
lives by our own growth and our
ability to help others grow.

ROBERT THEOBALD

When you combine classroom preparation, listening to the children, building trust and sharing feelings, you have opened the door to lifetime learning.

ELAINE YOUNG

Teachers recognize that the excitement of anxiety and challenge is the very zest of teaching. When they are involved and struggling, they do indeed feel most alive!

DR. HERBERT M. GREENBERG

If anything is going to happen,
teachers have to make it happen.

SANDY LENNING,
teacher at Denali Elementary,
Fairbanks, Alaska

I am a teacher, I love my work.
Educating, captivating the minds of
young people, fills me with a sense of
grand purpose. Every day is different.
My students intrigue and delight me
as their knowledge grows, as their
ideas germinate.

LAUNA ELLISON

If you plan for a year, plant a seed. If for ten years, plant a tree. If for a hundred years, teach the people. When you sow a seed once, you will reap a single harvest. When you teach people, you will reap a hundred harvests.

KUAN CHUNG

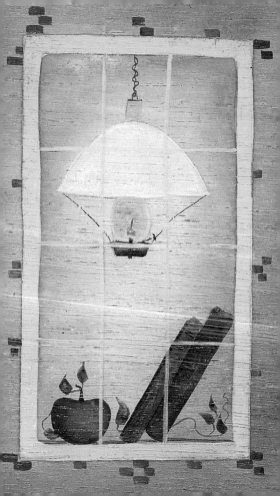

In high school, Ms. Winters taught us about the infinite world of the stars. At home most weekday afternoons, she shared with us the intricacies and pleasures of the piano. On Saturday mornings, she demonstrated to us the finer points of soccer. I have not become an astronomer; I don't often find the time to play the piano any more; and I didn't return to the soccer field until my own children lobbied me to be their coach. However, I am quick to tell you that Ms. Winters gave me the confidence to follow my own star, attuned my ear to listen for the music of life, and ingrained in me the patience and fortitude to be a nurturing parent to my own children.

EMMA LINN

I remember, at age 14, being intimidated at the beginning of Mr. Forand's 9th grade honors class in World History. The previous year's class told us that we had a better chance of winning the lottery than of getting an "A" on one of his tests. His first test was a shocker. Once we all knew what was expected, however, we did our darndest to meet his standard. Under Mr. Forand's expert tutelage and Socratic method of teaching, the class quickly became immersed in history from the richness of Ancient Greece and Rome right through to the 20th century.

We learned by memorization and lecture, but also through tactile learning facilitated by his use of ancient coins and even a two-handed broadsword! He showed slides of famous works of art, declaimed speeches, explained battle plans, and held impromptu discussions of any and all related topics. I have never met any other teacher so in love with his subject. He beguiled the entire class, and we not only made it through those impossible tests, but in fact excelled. Mr. Forand, you gave me a priceless gift—a lifetime love of learning.

CLAUDINE GANDOLFI

Every good teacher will learn more
about his subject every year—every
month, every week if possible.

GILBERT HIGHET

Teach the young people how to
think, not what to think.

SIDNEY SUGARMAN

The towering figure of Louise Bachelder dominated my Junior High years.

Miss Bachelder was almost six feet tall—unusual for a woman in the late 1940s—and by no means frail. She had an intense stare, and brooked no nonsense or backtalk. She was clear, direct, purposeful, and dedicated. We were at a minimum in awe of her, and at a maximum terrified. (I have recently run into former classmates who literally quaked in their boots at the mention of her name.)

Miss Bachelder had one primary professional goal, and that was to teach impressionable 7th to 9th graders the basic grammar and usage of both the

English and French languages. This she did with extraordinary skill and unrelenting pressure. I can still feel her stony gaze on me and my fellow pupils as we blurted out a wrong answer and then looked for some physical or emotional place to hide.

The results were amazing. Our first year French class entered three students in a County-wide exam, and they came in 1st, 2nd, and 5th. Perhaps it helped that we received an extra point on our term grade If we saw a movie in French!

Regrettably, Miss Bachelder was forced to retire in her late 50s after incurring two major heart attacks. She then

became a fond family friend, and was brought in by my mother to give her seal of approval to my fiancée (who, luckily, had been born in Paris). She edited 25 small volumes of quotations for the Peter Pauper Press and, to this day, as she nears 100 (her exact age is classified), makes keen observations about our newly-published titles.

I use the knowledge and love of words she instilled in me every day in my job as an editor. In my better moments, I reflect the positive attitude and high standards that she has always embodied. One teacher, one person, can make all the difference!

NICK BEILENSON

I was 14 years old when the space shuttle Challenger lifted off with America's first teacher in space on board. Our principal arranged for a TV to be placed in each classroom so that we could receive Ms. McAuliffe's lessons as they were beamed back to us. The morning of the launch we each sat in our seats in a state of anticipation. The countdown, as I remember it, went smoothly. The lift-off was a phantasmagoria of lights, flame, and energized sound. The Challenger rose and then veered, and there seemed to be a flash on the top right corner of the screen. There were sounds of panic coming from